POOL MAINTENANCE DIY BEGINNER'S GUIDE

THE ART OF KEEPING A CRYSTAL CLEAR POOL
ALL SEASON LONG WITH MINIMAL EFFORT

GABRIEL MARTIN

CONTENTS

Introduction	vii
1. KNOWING THE FUNDAMENTALS OF POOL MAINTENANCE	1
Importance Of Proper Pool Maintenance	2
Components Of A Swimming Pool	3
How Chemistry Affects Pool Maintenance	5
Common Pool Maintenance Technologies	7
Types of Swimming Pools	9
2. THE RIGHT EQUIPMENT AND CHEMICALS	14
Essential Pool Maintenance Equipment	14
Types of Water Testing	16
Types of Pool Chemicals And Their Functions	20
Safety Precautions When Handling Pool Chemicals	22
3. TASK ROUTINE FOR POOL MAINTENANCE	24
Skimming and Brushing the Pool	24
Emptying Baskets	25
Vacuuming The Pool	25
Checking and Adjusting Water Chemistry	25
Cleaning the Pool Filter	26
Skimmer Basket Cleaning	26
Steps to Clean the Pump Baskets	26
Maintaining the Water Level	27
Monitoring the Pool Temperature	28
4. COMMON TROUBLESHOOTING POOL PROBLEMS	29
Problem #1: Cloudy or Green Pool Water	30
Problem #2: Stains and Discolorations	30
Problem #3: Clogged Pool Filter	30

Problem #4: Poor Circulation   31
Problem #5: Low or High pH   31
Problem #6: Leaking Vinyl Liner   32
Problem #7: Pool Liner Coming Out of Track   33
Problem #8: Worn Out O-Ring   34

5. EXPLORING ADVANCED STRATEGIES FOR POOL MAINTENANCE   35
Shocking the Pool   35
Managing pH and Alkalinity Levels   37

6. EFFECTIVE MAINTENANCE FOR SALTWATER POOLS   45
Advantages and Disadvantages of Saltwater Pools   45
How Saltwater Pools Work   46
Maintaining the Saltwater Chlorine Generator   47
Balancing the Saltwater Chemistry   48
Common Saltwater Pool Maintenance Issues   49

7. PREPARING YOUR POOL FOR THE WINTER SEASON   52
Step One: Remove Accessories   53
Step Two: Deep Cleaning   53
Step Three: Balance Water Chemistry   53
Step Four: Lower Water Level   54
Step Five: Drain And Store Equipment   54
Step Six: Add Shock and Algaecide   55
Step Seven: Cover The Pool   55

8. ALGAE GROWTH CONTROL IN POOLS   56
Understanding Algae Growth in Pools   56
Types of Pool Algae (And How To Treat Them)   57
Preventing Algae Growth in Pools   58

9. WEEKLY TASKS   59
Clean Out Debris and Sediment   59
Clean The Skimmer(s)   60
Run Your Pump For Circulation   61

Check Filter And Backwash	62
Test Water And Adjust Chemistry	62
10. OPTIMIZING POOL MAINTENANCE FOR ENERGY EFFICIENCY	64
11. SEASONAL POOL CARE: MAINTAINING YOUR POOL THROUGHOUT THE YEAR	69
Opening Your Pool For The Season	69
Summer Maintenance Tasks	71
Winter Maintenance Tasks	72
12. ECO-FRIENDLY PRACTICES FOR POOL MAINTENANCE	73
Conclusion	79
Afterword	83
Resources	85

INTRODUCTION

So, you have a pool. Now what? Along the way, you've realized the significance of maintaining your pool. But what does that entail? And how do you accomplish it? What are the consequences if you neglect it?

Many individuals don't anticipate it, but owning and caring for a pool is a significant responsibility. You need to be prepared to ensure pool cleanliness, water balance, troubleshoot issues, and guarantee a healthy and safe environment for your enjoyment. It may seem like a substantial amount of work, and it certainly can be, but once you become familiar with the process, having a pool is truly remarkable.

Whether you've already got a pool or you're in the market for one, **Pool Maintenance DIY Beginner's Guide** *The Art of Keeping a Crystal Clear Pool All Season Long With Minimal Effort* is going to walk you through exactly what you need to do to take care of your pool.

Within this comprehensive guide, you will explore the intricacies of pool maintenance. By the conclusion, you will have a clear understanding of the precise steps required to ensure proper care for your pool, as well as the necessary actions to take in the event of any complications.

In Chapter 1, we will cover the basics of pool maintenance. This includes understanding why pool maintenance is important, what it entails, and what you can expect when maintaining your pool. In this chapter, we will also cover essential pool chemistry and the different types of swimming pools and how they ought to be cared for.

Moving on to Chapter 2, we delve into equipment and chemicals. Effectively caring for your pool necessitates specific equipment and chemicals to uphold cleanliness and maintain balanced water chemistry. It is crucial to pay careful attention to this chapter, as the handling of chemicals is vital for pool maintenance but can pose risks if not done correctly.

In Chapter 3, we will discuss routine pool maintenance tasks. This section encompasses activities such as skimming the pool, emptying baskets, and vacuuming the water. We will also discuss pool filters, pump baskets, and how to keep your pool full and the temperature perfect for swimming in.

In Chapter 4, we will discuss troubleshooting. This section aims to equip you with the necessary knowledge and skills to effectively address issues that may arise with your pool. Whether you encounter problems such as the pool turning green or cloudy, or notice any other abnormalities, this chapter will prepare you to handle them proficiently. We will also discuss equipment malfunctions so that, if something goes wrong, you can quickly identify and resolve the problem.

Chapter 5 delves into the realm of advanced pool maintenance techniques. This section is dedicated to understanding the crucial role of pH levels in maintaining your pool. Here, we will explore the process of water testing, deciphering the significance of the results, and acquiring the knowledge to safely and effectively utilize chemicals in order to adjust water chemistry levels as required. This chapter provides comprehensive guidance on achieving optimal pH balance for your pool.

In Chapter 6, we will discuss saltwater pools. Saltwater pools present a distinctive pool type with their own set of maintenance requirements. We will discuss the advantages and disadvantages of one, how they work, as well as how to take care of it properly.

Chapter 7 is dedicated to the vital process of winterizing your pool. Properly preparing your pool for the cold months is essential to prevent any inadvertent damage to its components. By effectively winterizing your pool, you ensure its longevity and enable yourself to enjoy it again in the upcoming springtime for many years to come.

In Chapter 8, we will delve into the topic of algae control. Pools sometimes encounter issues with algae growth, caused by the sun's exposure to the water, leading to algae formation within the pool water as well as on the pool walls and floor. We will provide guidance on what steps to take if you notice algae growth and how to restore the clarity of your pool water.

Moving on to Chapter 9, we will explore the essential weekly tasks required to maintain your pool. This chapter will present a comprehensive routine that you can follow to ensure proper water balance, maintain optimal temperature, ensure all pool technologies are in working order, and keep your pool ready for use at any time.

Chapter 10 will focus on seasonal care. Similar to the process of winterizing your pool, each season requires specific care measures due to varying weather conditions, temperatures, and levels of sunlight. We will discuss the unique considerations and maintenance practices necessary to keep your pool in optimal condition throughout different seasons.

To say this guide is comprehensive would be an understatement! But that's exactly why it's the perfect book for you. As a pool owner, you don't want to be left in the dark about what different chemicals are, how they work, or what your role is when it comes to taking care of your swimming pool.

You want your swimming pool to be clean, have crystal clear water, and remain enjoyable to use all season long for years to come. That's why this guide is the perfect sidekick for you: no matter what happens, you'll always know how to deal with it.

I suggest you first read this guide cover-to-cover, as it will give you an understanding of what to look out for. This way, if something is off, you'll be able to identify it immediately. You can then return to this text to figure out exactly what you need to do to take care of it and keep your pool clean, clear, and ready to use.

It would also be wise to keep this book handy so that, should anything arise, you can quickly check in and figure out what to do. This way, you are never at a loss for how to take care of your swimming pool.

With all that said, I'd say we are ready to dive into the world of pool maintenance! Let's go ahead and dig into this wonderful topic piece by piece so you're fully educated and ready to take care of your pool!

CHAPTER 1
KNOWING THE FUNDAMENTALS OF POOL MAINTENANCE

POOL MAINTENANCE *SOUNDS* like a massive task. In reality, it takes a bit to get your pool balanced but once it is it's quite simple to maintain. As long as you remain consistent, you will be able to quickly spot and treat imbalances so your pool is always ready-to-use. It is typically only when you are lenient with care that maintaining a pool can be troublesome.

In this chapter, we are going to discuss all the basics of pool maintenance so you clearly understand what it entails and what your role is in stabilizing and maintaining your pool properly. We will also explore the components of a swimming pool, water chemistry, common pool maintenance technologies, and types of swimming pools. By the end of this chapter you will have a complete understanding of the basics of taking care of your swimming pool.

IMPORTANCE OF PROPER POOL MAINTENANCE

Cleaning your swimming pool is important for a handful of reasons. First, it maintains the longevity of your pool and means you will face fewer costly repairs over time. By taking proper care of your pool, you ensure all parts are in good working order and issues don't go unnoticed to the point where they become extensive and costly.

In addition to keeping costs of maintenance low, proper pool maintenance ensures that your pool is functioning optimally. This means you will not have to work as hard to maintain it because each element of your pool and maintenance plan is doing a correct job.

Another benefit to keeping your pool properly maintained is that the water will remain safe to swim in. Many people do not realize that improperly maintained pools can be dangerous, as they can have improper pH levels or impurities that can cause serious issues for those that swim in it, ranging from burns or rashes to parasitic infections and various illnesses for anyone that swims in it. When your pool is properly maintained you can spend more time enjoying it and less time worrying about trying to take care of it and get it swimmable.

Finally, keeping your pool clean and maintained improves your property value if you own your home and increases the general aesthetic of your property. There is nothing pleasant or enjoyable about a dirty or unkempt pool. Further, if you were to sell your home, buyers would be cautious to avoid a poorly maintained pool because it could lead to costly repairs. Keeping your pool maintained ensures that it is both attractive and an asset to your property.

COMPONENTS OF A SWIMMING POOL

Standard swimming pools are made up of seven major components that help the pool run effectively. Each one plays a part in the pools proper operation. Let's look at each of these components and uncover what they are, how they work, and why they are important to the function of your swimming pool.

The Basin

The basin is the part of the pool that holds water. This is the part you swim in. When people think about a swimming pool, they are typically thinking about the basin. Very few think about the other components of the pool because they are devoted to maintaining the pool. The basin, however, *is* the pool. The basin can be above ground or below ground and can be designed in a number of different ways. Some are standard while others are custom made.

The Motorized Pump

The motorized pump is responsible for circulating water in your swimming pool. Still water is known for harboring a variety of different types of bacteria. It is also more desirable for parasites that lay their eggs in stagnant water. The motorized pump keeps the water circulating so that it is less likely to develop problems. Further, it ensures that anything you put in the pool, such as chemical cleaners, is evenly distributed throughout the water. Without the pump there would be no way to guarantee that the entire pool was circulated with anything you put in it.

The Water Filter

The water filter helps keep the water clean. It removes undesirable impurities like sand and dirt so that they don't end up in the pump or other mechanisms. If these impurities were not filtered out, the motorized mechanisms of the pool could become damaged because there would be debris built up in them. Keeping a fresh water filter in place ensures it is functioning optimally and that you are protecting your pool's technology from unnecessary damage.

The Chemical Feeder

The chemical feeder is a device that dispenses chemicals into your pool. Pool maintenance requires a variety of chemicals, such as chlorine and bromine, to keep the water safe to swim in. Chemicals are put in the chemical feeder and the feeder then dispenses them into the water. Some float while others are installed near the pump so that they can be dispensed into the water as the water is pumped out into the pool.

The Drains

The drains are responsible for draining water away from the basin and through the motorized pump so they can be purified by the water filter and circulated back into the pool. They are typically located on the bottom of the basin. These need to be kept clean of debris and in good working order so water can functionally drain out of the basin and circulate the system. If they are blocked, they can prevent the rest of the pool from working as it should and quickly lead to a build-up of debris, algae, bacteria, and other contaminants.

The Returns

The returns are typically located on the side of the basin and they are the portion of the pool that feeds water from the circulation system back into the basin. So, it drains through the drains, circulates through the motorized pump, then comes through the returns back into the basin. Like the drains, they need to remain free of blockages and debris so that water can safely make its way back into the pool.

The PVC Plastic Plumbing

The PVC plastic plumbing is responsible for connecting all of these different elements of your pool together. It runs from the drain to the filter, the filter to the pump, and the pump to the returns. The PVC plastic plumbing is typically set in sections and screwed together. This is partially so it can be made in any shape to effectively connect all of the components together. It is also because shorter lengths of PVC plastic plumbing pipes are easier to separate and clean out or service should any concerns arise with your pool.

HOW CHEMISTRY AFFECTS POOL MAINTENANCE

Chemistry in your swimming pool refers to the pH balance and purity of your water. A safe swimming pool needs to have a pH between 7 and 7.6 to ensure it is comfortable and safe to swim in. Anything higher can cause rashes, while anything lower can sting your eyes. You also need to ensure your pool is free of bacteria, algae, and other contaminants that can disrupt the water chemistry.

Apart from maintaining the pieces of your pool, your role when maintaining your pool is to maintain the water chemistry. You must take the right steps to ensure proper pH balance and water free of contaminants so that you can safely enjoy the pool. It is best to learn all you can about water chemistry and get into a good routine with checking and maintaining the chemistry of your pool. Well-maintained water is much less likely to come out of balance or be contaminated, and, if it does, can be quickly resolved since it has been properly maintained beforehand. Neglecting to take care of your water's chemistry can lead to imbalances and impurities that are both dangerous to swim in and difficult to get back under control.

How often you have to test and maintain your water chemistry depends on a few different factors. First, you want to consider how often the pool is being used. Water that is frequently swam in needs to be tested more frequently as it has a higher chance of coming out of balance. Aside from frequency, you also need to consider how many people and pets are using your swimming pool. Even if you only use your pool once a week or so, having several people and pets using it at the same time means you need to test the water more often.

Another thing that impacts your water testing is weather. Rain, high winds, and bouts of extreme heat or cold will affect your water chemistry. You must check after any of these conditions occur to ensure that no contaminants have been introduced to the pool and that the pH balances have not been impacted. Even if the pool doesn't look visibly contaminated, it could have had something introduced that affected the pH of your pool. For example, rainwater may not introduced contaminants to your pool, though it can. But even if it doesn't, it can change the pH of your pool because the pH balance of the rain might not be the same as your pool.

Finally, if you have had any recent fertilization or pest treatment done on or near your property you will want to check the water chemistry of your swimming pool. Even if it was not directly near the pool, these chemicals can contaminate your pool water and disturb your water chemistry. Checking in advance is an important means to avoid having a pool that is unsafe to swim in.

We will discuss this further in Chapter 5, but there will be five factors you are looking for in balanced water chemistry.

They include pH levels, total alkalinity, calcium hardness, temperature, and TDS (total dissolved solids.) All of these play a role in your water chemistry. How they are balanced also determines how you will treat the water to improve swimming conditions if you find that they are imbalanced upon testing.

COMMON POOL MAINTENANCE TECHNOLOGIES

Pools have been around for a long time. Because of this, many technologies exist that help you maintain your pool. Some will require more manual effort while others can do the job automatically. Regardless, you will have some level of involvement in looking after your equipment, maintaining your pool, and keeping it safe for swimming in.

You can greatly reduce the effort on your part, however, by investing in pool maintenance technologies. Be mindful that some technologies are more expensive to invest in, and all technologies will require their own maintenance to ensure they are in proper working order for your pool. This is important to consider when deciding which technologies will be right for you.

With that being said, there are five common pool maintenance technologies that you might invest in to help you maintain your pool. These are different from the standard pool maintenance tools we will discuss in Chapter 2, as they are typically more advanced. They include the following.

Automation Systems

Automation systems are used to automatically conduct a variety of different features on your pool. Some are designed to clean the pool, others will heat or cool it. Some automation systems light your pool and others still will filter or purify your water. This can be a great time-saving solution to keep your pool clean and usable without as much effort on your part. Keep in mind that automation systems can be more expensive to invest in and can require more expensive maintenance, too. Those who invest in them, however, typically feel they are well worth the investment.

Remote Controls

If you invest in automation, remote controls are another excellent investment. Automation systems may or may not come with remote controls as a part of the package. If they don't, you must physically walk over to the automation unit and select which setting you want to activate. With a remote control, however, you can conveniently control all aspects of the automation system from afar with the use of your remote control. Some automation systems come with apps you can install and use on your phone which is another great way to take care of your pool from afar.

Automatic Pool Cleaner

Automatic pool cleaners, unlike other automatic systems, are not built-in to your pool. Instead, they float in your swimming pool and automatically vacuum out any debris that has found its way into your pool. They can easily be removed from the water when you are using the pool or when you need to empty or maintain the system so it stays in good working order. They can also be physically brought indoors or stored somewhere safe during the off-season, if you have one, so they don't become damaged outdoors.

Ozone and Ultraviolet (UV) Purification Systems

An alternative to using chlorine and other chemicals to keep a safe water chemistry in your pool is using ozone and ultraviolet (UV) purification systems. These systems destroy a variety of organic contaminants and substantially reduce your need for chlorine. They are also known for neutralizing more disease-causing pathogens than chlorine can. It is worth noting that ozone purification systems and UV purification systems are two separate systems. I have mentioned them together, however, because they have been known to work best when used in tandem.

Heaters

Some people allow the sun to keep their pool warm. Their pool can be warmer or colder depending on the ambient temperature outside on a daily basis. An alternative is to install a water heater. Heaters allow you to keep the pool at a warmer, more enjoyable swimming temperature. If you like using your pool in cooler seasons this is especially helpful as it keeps the water warm enough to enjoy.

TYPES OF SWIMMING POOLS

There are many different types of swimming pools to choose from. If you are just in the market for one, you might feel a little intimidated by all the different options. Let's discuss what they are so you better understand what is out there and what will best fit your swimming pool needs.

Kiddie Pools

Kiddie pools are an excellent choice if you are looking for something safe and portable for your children to play in. They are typically inflatable, though some are made of hard plastic. They do not have all the different mechanical components of other pools and are generally much smaller. They are the most affordable pools on the market, though they also do not typically have the longevity of other pools.

Above-Ground Pools

Above-ground pools are both fully functional and affordable, making them an excellent choice for people that want a recreational swimming pool without spending an exorbitant amount on the cost. Another benefit of above-ground pools is that they tend to be easier to winterize and maintain in particularly cold climates compared to in-ground pools. They can often be disassembled and put away for the off-season so they are not being exposed to the elements. Further, you can DIY many of the components of the above-ground pool making it an even more affordable option if affordability is what you're looking for.

In-Ground Pools

In-ground pools are excellent for families that want something that will last. They are especially good for families that plan to use the pool frequently for recreational swimming. At one time, in-ground pools were reserved for luxury real estate because they costed so much to put in and, therefore, substantially increased the value of the property. These days, they can still increase property value but they are becoming more common in standard suburban neighborhoods.

Lap Pools

Lap pools are excellent for anyone looking for a health-oriented pool that is designed for exercising, not recreational purposes. They are typically long and narrow, so you can swim laps in them. If you are looking to do some fitness-level swimming and have a long, narrow space to put an in-ground pool in, a lap pool might be a great option.

Indoor Pools

Indoor pools are among the most expensive pools to put in your home. They require adequate space, as well as proper building materials to ensure the room doesn't become damaged from the humidity or water exposure caused by the pool. These pools average $65,000 to $85,000 or more and are not as common as backyard pools. They have the same maintenance requires as other pools, though they have an added bonus of being protected from the elements and contaminant exposure caused by being outdoors.

Architectural and Infinity Pools

Architectural and infinity pools are two varieties of pools that are both enjoyable for swimming while also being beautiful to look at. Architectural pools are often designed as a statement pool that can be built on virtually any property. Infinity pools are for properties that are built on a hill and have a view. They are designed with zero edge so you cannot see the structure of the pool when you look at it. They are designed to add to the beauty of the view and give the illusion of a waterfall, though no water is actually falling from the pool. These, like indoor pools, are significantly more expensive than basic in-ground or above-ground pools. If you have the means, however, they can be absolutely stunning and worth the investment. They substantially increase property value for whatever properties they are placed on.

· · ·

Natural Pools

Natural pools are excellent for swimming in while also giving a natural landscape appearance. They are self-cleaning pools that use water garden features to keep the water safe and hospitable for recreational swimmers. Typically, they are lined with rubber or polyethylene so the pool does not become contaminated with dirt. They can be designed to look however you desire and typically cost about the same as a standard in-ground pool.

Spools

Spools are designed for relaxation and socialization. They are typically too small for recreational swimming. Instead, they are similar to a hot tub, though they are larger and may be kept at cooler temperatures. They are excellent for cooling off on hot days, warming up on cool days, and socializing when you have friends over. Spools are occasionally built in-ground, but are more likely to be built as a part of a deck or another landscaping feature in your yard as an addition. They range from about $5,000 to $20,000 to build and are quite a bit easier to maintain than larger pools.

Saltwater Pools

Saltwater pools can be a great way to avoid chemical treatments as their water chemistry is maintained by the saltwater features, instead. They are quite popular in Australia and New Zealand, though they have become increasingly popular in North America. These are not an official design of pool, rather they represent a type of pool maintenance. Saltwater pools function by using a saltwater chlorine generator to convert bulk salt into natural chlorine. This chlorine then kills any bacteria and algae within the pool to keep it safe and hospitable for swimming. This feature can be applied to both in-ground and above-ground pools, but be aware that the generator itself must be built for the specific type of pool you have in order to be installed and functional.

Plunge Pools

Plunge pools are a type of alternative health pool that use cold water therapy as a health protocol. They are typically built as small square pools and are deep enough that you can submerge your entire body under water in them. They are often used before or after a heated workout or sauna or spa session as a way to cool the body down. It is said that this has therapeutic benefits. Plunge pools can be solo or they can be built as an addition to larger in-ground pools. They are quite deep so it is important that they are clearly marked and that people are safe around them to avoid accidental drowning, particularly with children.

CHAPTER 2
THE RIGHT EQUIPMENT AND CHEMICALS

YOU CAN DETERMINE which maintenance equipment and chemicals you need after you decide on the type of pool you have, since all pools have different requirements. Your pool maintenance equipment will consist of a variety of tools that clean the pool, as well as others that distribute chemicals to the pool. You will also need testing kits and chemicals to keep your water chemistry balanced. In this chapter, we will discuss all of these different types of equipment and chemicals so you can prepare your maintenance kit accordingly.

ESSENTIAL POOL MAINTENANCE EQUIPMENT

There are several different pieces of equipment you can use to maintain your pool. The following eight are the most important pieces of equipment that you should have on-hand when you are building your pool maintenance kit.

Pool Vacuum

Pool vacuums are a special type of vacuum that can be submerged into the pool to clean debris and sediment out of your pool. They are generally used to clean the bottom of the pool where sediment and other debris can build up and create a dirty pool floor.

Pool Net
Pool nets can refer to two pieces of equipment. The first is a maintenance tool which we will talk about, while the second is a net that physically covers the pool to avoid accidental drownings with children or pets. Pool nets, the maintenance tool, are used to remove things like leaves from the pool.

Pool Skimmer
Unlike the pool net, the pool skimmer is a more shallow piece of mesh that is used to scrape the surface of the pool. It removes finer debris like sediment that is floating in your pool. Some tools have attachments that enable it to double as a net *and* a skimmer and tend to come cheaper than purchasing the two devices separately.

Pool Brush
A pool brush helps scrub the bottom and sides of your pool. Typically, you will brush the pool either before or between vacuuming the pool so you can loosen debris and sediment to then be cleaned by the vacuum.

Gloves
Gloves are an essential piece of safety equipment when working with the pool. In particular, pool chemicals can be harsh on your skin. Some can even be corrosive when they are not being diluted by the pool water. Wearing gloves when working with any chemical is an important part of protecting yourself.

Eye Protection
Like with gloves, eye protection is an important part of staying safe while testing and adjusting water chemistry.

Proper plastic wrap around goggles that completely cover your eyes is important to avoid accidental splashing or loose particles from blowing into your eyes and causing damage.

Water Test Kit

Water test kits allow you to check your water chemistry. The results of your test kits will determine how you proceed with maintaining your pool, such as which chemicals you will use or how you will reduce or increase chemical usage to create a desirable outcome.

Chemical Feeder

Chemical feeders, as described in chapter 1, are essential in pool maintenance as they enable you to administer chemicals in the water. Not all pools require them. However, those that do will require you to have one on hand so you can introduce chemicals to your water to maintain or rebalance the chemistry as needed.

TYPES OF WATER TESTING

Your water chemistry is defined by a variety of factors. Because of this, there are a variety of test kits you will be using to test your pool for safe usage. In general, there are seven different types of tests you will need to be aware of to ensure your pool is in good working order. I have described each one and its uses below.

Standard Pool Test Kits

Standard pool test kits are designed to help you get a complete read on how your pool is doing. They are more time consuming than test strips because rather than focusing on just one element of your pools chemistry they focus on many.

There are two types of pool test kits: DPD tests and OTO-Phenol test kits. DPD kits typically measure chlorine, pH,

THE RIGHT EQUIPMENT AND CHEMICALS

alkalinity, stabilizer, and water hardness. OTO-Phenol kits test for only chlorine and pH. DPD test kits are typically better because they give a broader understanding of what is going on with your pool's chemistry. However, OTO-Phenol kits can be useful for combining chlorine and pH testing if you are doing specialty readings.

There are five steps to using a pool test kit. They include:

1. Removing the caps and rinsing the test tubes before using the kit.
2. Filling the tubes with pool water until they reach the built-in indicator lines. It is important to extract your water sample from elbow-depth water away from the jets if your pool has any.
3. Once the tube is filled, follow the directions exactly as described on the package. This includes dropping the appropriate amount of reagent solution into the water sample.
4. Next, you will cap the tube and shake gently to ensure the solution is thoroughly combined.
5. Lastly, you will compare the color of water in the tube to the chart provided in your test kit.

The color of your water will determine how balanced your chemistry is. If it is imbalanced you will need to use appropriate chemicals to achieve balance once again.

Specialty Tests for Your Pool

Specialty tests are smaller tests that check for just one aspect of your pool's chemistry or usability. They may come in the form of strips or, in the case of water temperature, a thermometer. These tests can help you get a better understanding of your pools chemistry and whether or not it will be safe or enjoyable to swim in. If you notice something is off with these kits, you can take the necessary steps to balance that aspect of your pool's water chemistry.

Chlorine Testing

Free chlorine is the amount of water that is built up in your pool. Maintaining adequate chlorine levels is essential to avoid the growth of algae and bacteria. You need to use this test kit two to three times per week. An ideal reading is 1 to 4 parts per million (ppm.)

Calcium Hardness Testing

Calcium hardness leads to scale buildup in your pool and pool's hardware and technology. It can also corrode the equipment in your pool. You should test for calcium hardness once per month to ensure it remains in the ideal range of 175 to 275 ppm.

Temperature Testing

The temperature of your pool helps determine if it will be enjoyable to swim in. A simple thermometer will suffice and you can keep your pool at a temperature that is enjoyable for you and anyone else that uses your pool. An ideal temperature is less than 82 degrees, as anything warmer can impact your comfort when swimming.

. . .

THE RIGHT EQUIPMENT AND CHEMICALS 19

Total Dissolved Solids (TDS) Testing

TDS can be tested with a strip or a digital test meter. The digital test meter is more accurate but strips are enough for most swimming pool needs. Too must TDS in your water can lead to cloudy, dull water, poor filtration, chronically imbalanced chlorine levels despite shocking your water, algae and scale growth, and salty water that leaves crusty deposits when it evaporates. TDS levels should be lower than 2500 ppm. If they are higher, you might need to drain and refill your pool to gain a better reading and clearer, more enjoyable, and safer water chemistry.

pH Testing

Improper pH levels can lead to discomfort causing skin rashes or itchy or burning eyes or other issues when people use your pool. You want to maintain a balance between 7.2 to 7.6 pH to ensure your water is safe and comfortable to swim in. You should test your pH two to three times per week and use a pH adjuster as needed to maintain proper balance.

Cyanuric Acid Testing

Cyanuric acid is essential for regulating chlorine levels in your pool. If you do not have enough cyanuric acid in your pool the sunlight will cause your chlorine to be consumed too quickly, meaning the chlorine doesn't have enough time to be effective and you end up consuming more chlorine in your pool maintenance than is necessary. Too much and it can lock up your chlorine and prevent it from sanitizing your pool adequately. You want your cyanuric acid levels to be between

30 and 50 ppm in a regular pool or 60 and 80 ppm in a saltwater pool.

Algaecide, Stabilizer, Phosphates, and Nitrates Testing

Stabilizer, algaecide, phosphates, and nitrates are all different specialty chemicals that achieve different goals in your pool. Stabilizer helps extend the life of chlorine and algaecide helps remove algae. You don't want too much of either in your pool or it can be harmful to the pool's users. Phosphates and nitrates grow in your pool as a result of poor water chemistry or decaying organic matter in your pool, such as leaves. Both can encourage the growth of algae, turn your pool green, and require you to need substantially more chlorine to maintain safe swimming conditions.

TYPES OF POOL CHEMICALS AND THEIR FUNCTIONS

There are many different chemicals that you will use to cleanse, stabilize, and balance your pool's water chemistry. There are six that you will use on a consistent basis to ensure your pool is safe and usable. They include: chlorine, bromine, oxidizers, cyanuric acid, pH increaser/decreaser, and alkalinity adjusters.

Chlorine

Chlorine is used to sanitize your pool. It operates as an algaecide and oxidizes undesirable contaminants. It is the "all-in-one" pool cleanser that keeps your water safe to swim in. Every other chemical you use in your pool will be to ensure that the chlorine can do it's job effectively. Chlorine is added to pools regularly to keep the levels between 1 and 3 ppm. It is tested for two to three times per week.

• • •

Bromine

Bromine is similar to chlorine in that it is used to sanitize your pool, but it is more stable than chlorine is indoors. It is also more effective in high-heat environments, such as hot tubs. With that being said, the UV from the sun will destroy bromine which means it doesn't last as long outdoors. It is less common in swimming pools and more common in spa-like settings or indoor pools.

Oxidizers

Oxidizers are nonchlorine sanitization chemicals that work as a secondary solution alongside chlorine. Occasionally, they are added to shock the pool to help chlorine break down organic contaminants when the chlorine alone is not doing enough work. It is best to use these in the evening or at night so the sun's UV rays don't destroy the oxidizer before it can work.

Cyanuric Acid

Cyanuric acid is used to help chlorine last longer. On its own, chlorine can burn off quickly due to the UV rays caused by the sun. With cyanuric acid the chlorine lasts longer meaning you do not have to add so much chlorine. Many types of chlorine tablets have cyanuric acid built-in, but this is not advised. These tablets do not allow you to adjust cyanuric acid levels and too little or too much can result in improper chlorine use that damages your pool. It is better to be able to control the two independently to achieve the right results for your pools unique water chemistry.

. . .

pH Increaser/Decreaser

pH levels are essential to enable your pool chemicals to do their job while also keeping your water safe to swim in. If you test your pool's pH and it is too high, you need to add pH decreaser to achieve a safer level. If it is too low, you need to use pH increaser to achieve safer levels. Often, soda ash is used to increase pool pH, while sodium bisulfate or muriatic acid is used to quickly drop your pools pH level. It is important not to use too much of either, otherwise you could swing your pool in the opposite direction and cause the opposite problem. It is better to use a little at a time until you get the desired result than to overdo it and swing back and forth.

Alkalinity Adjusters

Alkalinity is another element that helps your pool maintain proper pH levels. If your water is murky there is a good chance that your pools pH levels are imbalanced. Alkalinity adjuster can help you lower or increase your water's alkalinity quickly. To increase total alkalinity (TA), you can use sodium bicarbonate anytime it falls below 100 ppm. Muriatic acid helps lower TA.

SAFETY PRECAUTIONS WHEN HANDLING POOL CHEMICALS

It is essential that you handle and store pool chemicals properly to avoid accidental hazards that can be caused by improper chemical use or storage. First and foremost, keep all chemicals out of the reach of children and pets who could be severely injured by touching or consuming pool chemicals. You also need to keep your chemicals in a cool, dry location with good ventilation. They also need to be kept away from heat and electrical sources.

Each chemical should be contained properly and sealed and stored off the ground but close to the floor to avoid hazards from the chemicals falling. Liquid and solid chemicals should always be stored separately.

When you use your pool chemicals, do so in a well-ventilated area to avoid being harmed by exposure or ingestion. Also, be very careful when introducing new chemicals to your pool. Certain chemicals should never be mixed as they can cause serious risk if they are. For example, muriatic acid and chlorine can form dangerous chlorine gasses when mixed which can cause injuries or fatalities.

You should always have goggles, gloves, and a mask on when using pool chemicals to avoid burns, accidental ingestion, or inhalation of chemicals. This will also protect you against accidental splashes that could cause serious injuries.

Each pool chemical you purchase will have a Material Data Safety Sheet (MSDS) provided. Refer to that to ensure you are handling pool chemicals properly.

CHAPTER 3
TASK ROUTINE FOR POOL MAINTENANCE

YOUR POOL REQUIRES routine maintenance tasks that keep it clean, clear, and safe to swim in. We have already covered a lot of the expectations you should have about keeping your pool safe to swim in. Now, we are going to break these tasks down into an easy-to-follow weekly routine of pool maintenance tasks that will help you look after your pool properly.

Each task in this chapter is something you need to be doing every week to keep your pool in good operational order and to keep the water safe for swimming.

SKIMMING AND BRUSHING THE POOL

Ideally, you should be skimming your pool daily to remove organic matter such as fallen leaves and debris from your pool. This way, they do not break down and disrupt your water chemistry. You should brush your pool weekly to ensure that no sediment, algae, or dirt has built up in your pool. Brush the sides, bottom, the ladder, and any other fixtures in your pool to ensure nothing is left behind causing problems for your water chemistry.

EMPTYING BASKETS

The baskets in your pool work to help remove organic matter and debris from your pool, as well. This is like a double-up on the manual skimming you should be doing daily. At least once a week, but ideally daily, you should be emptying the baskets to ensure no debris remains in your pool disrupting your water chemistry.

VACUUMING THE POOL

After brushing your pool, allow the algae and sediment a moment to sink to the bottom of the pool. Then, vacuum them out. This ensures that they are not simply moved around the pool but that they are completely removed instead. If you are using an automatic vacuum, plug in your cleaner, put it in the water and let your automatic vacuum do the job for you.

CHECKING AND ADJUSTING WATER CHEMISTRY

Chlorine and pH need to be tested at least two to three times per week. Other tests are typically done once per month or when you notice an imbalance in chlorine or pH and need to identify why. It is essential that you routinely check your water chemistry and adjust it as needed with the appropriate chemicals for the job. Maintaining your water on a consistent basis ensures that imbalances are treated quickly so they do not fester and become more problematic to treat.

CLEANING THE POOL FILTER

It is important to check and clean your pool filter once per week to avoid debris from building up and damaging your filter or other parts of your pool. If needed, backwash your filter to dislodge any debris. It is important that it remains as clean as possible so it can stay in good working order and protect the rest of your pool's plumbing and technology from damage.

SKIMMER BASKET CLEANING

Skimmer baskets should be cleaned once per week, too. These baskets, like the other baskets in your pool, help collect sediment and debris that has fallen into your water. Keeping them clean ensures they continue to do a good job and that any debris that has been gathered does not break down in the water and contribute to imbalanced water chemistry levels.

STEPS TO CLEAN THE PUMP BASKETS

It is important to keep your pump running long enough each day to ensure that water is properly filtered through your pool and the circulation system remains in good working condition.

You also need to clean the pump baskets. This is an important process that requires a series of steps to be taken to ensure it is done correctly.

These steps include:

1. Turning off power to the pool pump.
2. Relieving built-up pressure by turning the air relief

valve on top of the filter counterclockwise and letting it decrease to 0 psi.
3. Removing the pump lid
4. Removing, cleaning, and inspecting the basket.
5. Inspecting the pump lid. Replacing the pool pump and lid.
6. Turning the power back onto the pump.
7. Closing the air relief valve by turning it clockwise. It should get back to a reading of 15-20 psi.

MAINTAINING THE WATER LEVEL

Your water should always be kept at the halfway point of your skimmer hatch, which is the hatch that sits on the side of your in-ground pool. It should sit no lower than one-third of the height of your skimmer hatch.

If your water level is too low you must immediately take action to refill the water because a lack of water can cause costly damage to your pool. As your skimmer hatch draws air into the filtration system it can damage the skimmer hatch itself as well as to the pump and filtration system. High water levels are not as serious as low water levels but they can still place excess demand on your skimmer and filtration system causing damage to it.

From time to time, you might have to add or remove water to your pool to keep it at a safe level. This will be more likely during hot spells when water evaporates faster or during rainy spells where your pool collects excess rainwater.

You should keep an eye on your water levels daily to ensure they are at an ideal range.

MONITORING THE POOL TEMPERATURE

Lastly, you want to monitor pool temperature. The easiest way to do this is to invest in a wireless pool thermometer that hooks up to an app on your smartphone and allows you to monitor pool temperature remotely. Additionally, these devices can alert you if your pool becomes too hot or too cold.

Ideally, your pool should remain between 75 and 85 degrees Fahrenheit. This way, the chlorine lasts longer and other pool chemicals are not as necessary.

There are two common ways to heat your pool. The first is using a gas pool heater to warm your water. The second is using a solar cover. In some cases, both will be necessary to keep your pool warm enough.

If your pool gets too hot, you can use fountains and waterfalls, drains, shade, and reversible heat pumps to help cool your pool down. Typically, high water temperatures are less common than lower ones because it takes a lot for an entire pool's worth of water to warm up to high temperatures.

CHAPTER 4
COMMON TROUBLESHOOTING POOL PROBLEMS

NEW POOL OWNERS might feel panicked the first time they run into a problem with their pool. As long as everything remains balanced and stable, your pool is fun and enjoyable. When something goes wrong, it can feel overwhelming and confusing to know what to do to get it back under control.

Once you've dealt with a problem, dealing with it a second or third time if it happens again is no problem. If this is your first time, however, you might be feeling intimidated by the problem and the solutions you must implement to get your pool back to being safe and enjoyable.

In this chapter, we are going to cover common pool problems that you might face and what you should do in the event they occur in your pool. By the end, you should be feeling a lot more confident in maintaining your pool regardless of what conditions arise. Further, this chapter is particularly important to keep nearby in case a problem does arise with your pool. You might even want to print it out and keep it near your pool testing kits and maintenance tools to ensure you can refer back to it whenever needed.

PROBLEM #1: CLOUDY OR GREEN POOL WATER

If you notice your pool has turned a shade of green, chances are you have algae growing in your pool. This often happens if you've skipped testing your water and the chlorine levels have dropped too low in your pool. This can also happen if your chlorine is being consumed too quickly, such as by UV exposure or poor water temperatures. In chapter 8, we will go deeper into algae control.

In the meantime, the best thing to do is to do a full pool test kit and identify where your water chemistry is sitting. Add chemicals as needed to regain balance and clean your water of any algae or bacteria that has built up in your pool.

PROBLEM #2: STAINS AND DISCOLORATIONS

Some types of algae are yellow or brown in color and can stain your pool. These stains do not necessarily indicate that algae growth is present, but they can be ugly and unsightly. The best way to remove algae stains is to apply chlorine straight onto the discoloration and scrub it in with a brush. You should also run a pool water test to see if there is any imbalance that could be causing the algae to continue growing and discoloring your pool or staining the liner.

PROBLEM #3: CLOGGED POOL FILTER

You need to clean your filter at least once per week to keep it clean and operational. If you have cloudy or green water, check your pool filter to ensure nothing has gotten stuck in it which could be disrupting the water chemistry in your pool.

If your filter is completely clogged, take the steps described in Chapter 3 and remove the filter for proper cleaning. Often, backwashing is plenty to remove any clogs from your filter and get it back in good working condition.

PROBLEM #4: POOR CIRCULATION

Clogged pool filters are the most common issue for poor circulation in your pool. However, there are other concerns that can lead to poor circulation.

The two most common reasons are that you have blown a fuse or have an electrical problem, or that you have a hole in the airline which prevents it from functioning properly and therefore stops your pool from circulating water.

If you are positive that your filter is not responsible for poor circulation it is important to get a pool repair company out straight away to fix a possible electrical or airway issue. These can be either dangerous, costly, or both if they are left unresolved.

PROBLEM #5: LOW OR HIGH PH

As I have mentioned a few times throughout this guide now, the safest pH level for your swimming pool is a reading between 7.2 and 7.6. If your pH is off, you can experience a range from problems from rashes to irritation of the eyes and throat caused by the acidity of your pool and the possible growth of harmful bacteria.

If you test your pool and discover the pH balance is off, you will need to balance the pH using pH increaser or decreaser. These chemicals should be used sparingly, as too much of them can swing your chemistry in the opposite direction. Once you have put them in the water, wait a few hours for them to circulate throughout the pool and then test your pH balance again.

If you find your pH balance consistently goes off, it might be worth checking your overall chemical maintenance approach to ensure you are adding adequate chemicals at the right times to maintain optimal pool chemistry.

PROBLEM #6: LEAKING VINYL LINER

Pools feature vinyl liners that coat the basin to ensure that water does not leak through the basin and into the ground. If your pool's water level goes down by ¼ to ½ inch, this is likely caused by evaporation. Anything more than that, however, could be the result of a leak. Leaks require immediate action as they can be detrimental to the pool's circulation system. Further, they can cause problems in your groundwater and introduce unwanted bacteria into your pool water.

The first thing you need to do if your water levels are going down too much is check the piping and pool equipment to ensure there is not a leak in those systems. Assuming the connections are tight and no leak is identified, you will need to check the liner to locate the source of the leak.

If your water level has stabilized, meaning it is not still leaking, your leak is likely located at or around the water level. If it continues to leak, you will need to check the lower parts of the liner or the floor of the pool to see if you can locate where the leak is happening. Once you find the leak, use duct tape to temporarily repair it. Duct tape is effective at holding your liner together, even underwater, though it will not hold your pool together for long. Once it's in place, you must quickly work to repair the leak properly so it does not reoccur.

There are two ways to repair a leak in your vinyl liner. The first is to replace the entire liner. If your liner is more than ten years old and is particularly worn out in one or more areas, this is advisable as leaks will become more prevalent the older your liner gets. If your liner is younger and is in otherwise great shape, a patch might be sufficient to restore the liner so you can continue to use your pool. Patches can last several years with no problems, so this is worth a try for newer liners.

PROBLEM #7: POOL LINER COMING OUT OF TRACK

As your pool liner gets older, it runs the risk of coming out of track. This occurs as the material becomes stiffer and, therefore, less stretchy. It also begins to shrink over time. Typically, liners will begin to pull away at the corners first. You may be able to repair this for a time by boiling a large amount of water and pouring it directly onto the spot where the vinyl is pulling away from the corner. The hot water will make the vinyl more pliable, meaning you can re-stretch it to get it back in the track. Be careful, as the boiling water will make the vinyl too hot to touch at first. After a few seconds, however, it will be cool enough that you can pull it back into place before it cools down and becomes unworkable again.

You might need to redo this several times to get the entire vinyl liner back into place. It is essential that you are thorough and leave nothing out of the track, as anything left unattached will result in the liner immediately coming loose again beginning at that point.

If your pool liner is older, or if the space where it is pulling is too large to reattach, you will need to call in professionals to repair the liner. Chances are, they will replace the liner if it is old or the area where it has come loose is too large, since repairing a liner in this condition will not last.

PROBLEM #8: WORN OUT O-RING

Your pool's pump and filter both have O-rings on them that keep them working efficiently. If one becomes worn out, it will need to be replaced as it will lead to leaking which can cause extensive damage to your pool equipment.

To replace your O-rings, purchase replacements as well as a silicone-based lubricant. Apply the lubricant to the O-ring before you install it, as this will extend its life so you don't have to replace them as often. Keeping up with this simple maintenance task can save you a substantial amount of money over time, so be sure to check on your equipment frequently and replace O-rings and other replaceable parts as needed.

CHAPTER 5
EXPLORING ADVANCED STRATEGIES FOR POOL MAINTENANCE

OCCASIONALLY, your pool will require more advanced maintenance. This typically occurs if the pool has not been frequently maintained and has been allowed to develop severely unbalanced water chemistry, or if you are setting the pool up again after having it drained or out of service for any period.

The more advanced pool maintenance techniques you might have to deal with largely revolve around pH levels and water chemistry. In this chapter, we will go deeper into how to check for and maintain your pH levels properly and what to do if they are consistently out of balance and need to be restored.

SHOCKING THE POOL

Sometimes, your pool's chemistry will become so imbalanced that you need to shock the water. This is typically done when your free chlorine level is too low and, as a result, a variety of unwanted conditions are surfacing, such as algae, chloramine, and bacteria levels increasing to undesirable levels. Shocking your pool will quickly kill off these unwanted contaminants so you can once again balance your pool's water chemistry and enjoy swimming in it.

It is worth noting that just because your pool smells like chlorine doesn't mean your chlorine levels are high. In fact, this could indicate that the water needs to be shocked. A clean pool should not have much of a smell at all. A pool that smells like chlorine likely actually smells like chloramine, which is also known as combined chlorine. This is caused by sweat, oils, and urine mixing with chlorine in the pool and giving off an undesirable odor. With that being said, smell alone does not indicate that your pool needs to be shocked. You will need to conduct a water test to see if your pool's chlorine levels are off or if it needs to be shocked.

Some signs that indicate your pool needs to be shocked include:

- Algae is growing in your pool
- The free chlorine level has measured at zero
- Your chloramine or combined chlorine levels are over 0.5 ppm

If you suspect you need to shock your pool, always test your water first. If you are indeed correct that you need to shock it, purchase shock and refer to the package for how much to mix into your pool and how to safely mix it into your pool's water. Some pool shock comes in the form of granules and can be added to the pool directly; however, this is not as common as the varieties that need to first be diluted with water before adding it to your pool. You can also buy liquid pool shock, which is prediluted and ready to be added to the pool at any time.

Before you shock your pool, always make sure the pump is running. As well, ensure you are using proper safety equipment, including gloves and safety glasses, before opening or using any pool chemicals. Then, add the shock around the edges of the pool and let the pump run for at least six hours, but preferably longer. Around six to eight hours after you shock your pool, test the water to see if you have proper chlorine levels. Never use the pool immediately after shocking it. Instead, wait until the free chlorine level drops to between 1 to 3 ppm.

MANAGING PH AND ALKALINITY LEVELS

In chapter 2, we discussed the importance of checking for pH and alkalinity in your pool's water chemistry. These, in addition to free chlorine levels, are essential to keep an eye on as they can have a substantial impact on the quality of your pool's water. In chapter 5, you discovered how serious this can be if the pH of your water is abnormal.

In this chapter, we are going to discuss *how* to test for pH and what to do if you discover that your pH levels are abnormal. We will also discuss regular pH level maintenance so you can avoid having your pH levels become abnormal in the first place.

Note that if your pH is off, this means your water alkalinity is off. Too high of a pH means your water has become too alkaline, while too low of a pH makes your water too acidic.

• • •

How to Test for pH

Testing your pool for pH is simple. All you need is a pH test strip kit. You simply dip the test strip into your pool water and then wait a few moments for it to change color. A good quality pH test kit will come with a color chart that helps you determine the pH level of your water by comparing the color of the strip to the chart.

Problems Caused By A High pH

If you test your water and discover the pH is over 7.8, you will need to lower the pH immediately. Too high of a pH can lead to a handful of problems for both the water chemistry and the people that are using your swimming pool.

For water chemistry, too high of a pH means your pool is too alkaline. These conditions prevent your chlorine from working properly which means harmful pathogens can grow in your water. These pathogens can further damage water chemistry levels while also introducing bacteria that could lead to injuries, infections, or illnesses for anyone swimming in your pool. Scaling and cloudy water are also common when water is too alkaline since the chlorine cannot effectively kill off the pathogens leading to these concerns in the first place.

Alkaline water itself can cause issues for humans, as well. If pH is too high, swimming in that water can lead to a variety of skin rashes. Some of these come from the pathogens within the pool while others are caused by the water itself being irritating to your skin.

How to Lower Your Pools pH

If you test your pool water and discover that the pH is too high, you will need to reduce the alkalinity of your pool water before using it again. There is a chemical that is ready for pool use which is called "pH reducer" or "pH minus." This chemical uses either muriatic acid or sodium bisulfate (aka 'dry acid') to reduce the alkalinity in your pool water. Pool supply stores and most home improvement stores will have these chemicals available for you to purchase.

It is essential that you use proper safety equipment and are careful not to get pH reducer or pH minus on your body as it is highly caustic and can cause serious acid burns. To give you an idea of how powerful these chemicals are, muriatic acid is used to etch concrete. It is incredibly dangerous if it comes into contact with your skin, respiratory system, eyes, or other body parts. Typically, muriatic comes in liquid form so the biggest danger is accidental spills or splashes. Sodium bisulfate comes in granules and is typically safer to handle, however it can still be dangerous particularly to your respiratory system.

You will need to follow the guide on your pH reducer compound to ensure you add the right amount to your pool as the amount you add will vary depending on the water volume in your pool and its current pH reading. Be sure to follow the guide carefully to avoid adding too many chemicals to your pool and creating an acidic water chemistry.

Problems Caused By A Low pH

If your water pH is too low, this mean your pool water is acidic. Anything lower than 7.2 needs to be addressed immediately to avoid causing problems with your pool's equipment as well as anyone swimming in your pool.

To your pool equipment, a low pH can corrode your equipment and cause it to break down. It can also damage the finish of your pool's liner and burn through your chlorine faster than your pool water should. It is essential that you raise the pH quickly if you find it is too low to avoid having your pool equipment damaged by the acidic water quality.

Anyone that swims in your pool is at risk, too, if the pH is too acidic. It can cause your skin to itch and cause your eyes to sting. In rare cases, if your water is too acidic, it can also lead to skin burns. The trouble with pH is that human skin typically has a pH of between 5.4 to 5.9 which means we can handle rather acidic pool water before it becomes problematic. By the time you begin to feel the effects of acidic water, it has already dropped considerably and needs to be rectified immediately.

How to Increase Your Pools pH

If you notice your pools pH has dropped too low, it's time to use pH increaser. Soda ash and baking soda are two things commonly used to increase pH. Before you add either to your pool, however, it is essential that you know how much water your pool holds so you know how much to add to it. Adding too much can cause your pool to become too alkaline and will require you to then increase the acidity.

Online, you can find pool volume calculators that help you determine the volume of water your pool holds. Typically, they work by inputting the length and width of the pool as well as the depth at the shallow end and the depth at the deep end. By taking these metrics into account they can let you know how much water you have in your pool so you know how much chemicals to add when you are correcting your water chemistry. *Swim University* has a great calculator on their website that you can use if needed.

Once you know your pool's volume you can use the following chart to determine how much baking soda to add to your pool to increase its alkalinity.

	Volume Of Water In Your Pool			
To Increase pH by (ppm)	5,000 Gallon pool	10,000 Gallon pool	15,000 Gallon pool	20,000 Gallon pool
10 ppm	0.75 pounds of baking soda	1.5 pounds of baking soda	2.25 pounds of baking soda	3.0 pounds of baking soda
20 ppm	1.5 pounds of baking soda	3.0 pounds of baking soda	4.5 pounds of baking soda	6.0 pounds of baking soda
30 ppm	2.25 pounds of baking soda	4.5 pounds of baking soda	6.75 pounds of baking soda	9.0 pounds of baking soda
40 ppm	3.0 pounds of baking soda	6.0 pounds of baking soda	9.0 pounds of baking soda	12.0 pounds of baking soda
50 ppm	3.75 pounds of baking soda	7.5 pounds of baking soda	11.25 pounds of baking soda	15.0 pounds of baking soda
60 ppm	4.5 pounds of baking soda	9.0 pounds of baking soda	13.0 pounds of baking soda	18.0 pounds of baking soda
70 ppm	5.25 pounds of baking soda	10.5 pounds of baking soda	15.75 pounds of baking soda	21.0 pounds of baking soda
80 ppm	6.0 pounds of baking soda	12.0 pounds of baking soda	18.0 pounds of baking soda	24.0 pounds of baking soda
90 ppm	6.75 pounds of baking soda	13.5 pounds of baking soda	20.25 pounds of baking soda	27.0 pounds of baking soda
100 ppm	7.5 pounds of baking soda	15.0 pounds of baking soda	22.5 pounds of baking soda	30.0 pounds of baking soda

Controlling Calcium Hardness in Your Water

Twice per year, you should test the calcium hardness in your pool water. If you live somewhere that calcium hardness tends to be a larger problem, or you frequently measure high, increase your testing to every third month or even every other month to ensure you are not letting calcium hardness build up too much in your pool.

Calcium hardness tests use two different reagents to change the color of pool water from red to blue to determine how much calcium hardness is present in your water. You will multiply the amount of drops you added of the *second* reagent to determine how much calcium hardness is in your water. The exact equation for this will be indicated on the instruction manual for your test kit. You want your calcium hardness to be between 175 ppm and 225 ppm for optimal range if you have a vinyl or fiberglass liner. If you have a concrete or plaster pool, you want a range between 200 ppm and 275 ppm.

If your calcium hardness tests high you will need to reduce your calcium hardness. Often, you can tell you have calcium hardness in your pool because the water becomes cloudy. Shocking your pool is often the first thing people do when they notice cloudiness in their water, but if the shock doesn't work it may be due to calcium hardness. Shocking your pool will not eliminate cloudiness caused by calcium hardness.

The fastest way to reduce calcium hardness is to drain and replace about half of the water in your pool. Before you do, be sure to test your water source so you do not accidentally add more calcium hardness into your pool through your filling source since this would obviously not resolve your problem.

If you can't or don't want to drain some of your water, or

if your source has high calcium hardness, too, try using pool flocculant. Also known as floc, this substance clumps the excess calcium together and drops it to the bottom of the pool. If you use this, it is essential that you turn your pool filter off and vacuum the floc out of the bottom of your pool before turning it back on. Not doing this will destroy your filter as the clumps will damage the entire mechanism.

Lastly, muriatic acid can be useful in eliminating calcium hardness levels by raising the saturation of your pool which can bring your water back into balance. This should be a last resort option, as it does not actually remove calcium hardness from your pool.

If you find you are on the opposite end of the spectrum and your water is too soft you must raise your calcium hardness levels. You might think this is not a problem, but the reality is that water that is too soft can be corrosive to your pool by dissolving concrete and plaster and corroding metal components underwater in your pool. You can easily raise calcium hardness levels by simply adding calcium hardness increaser to your pool. You will need to follow the instructions on your specific calcium hardness increaser to ensure you follow the correct steps and bring your pool back into balance.

To avoid your calcium hardness becoming imbalanced ensure you keep your pool clean, keep the water balanced, test frequently, and address any imbalances early. Allowing imbalances to build up over time causes more problems in the long run and will be harder to remedy as time goes on and the imbalance grows stronger a

CHAPTER 6
EFFECTIVE MAINTENANCE FOR SALTWATER POOLS

IF YOU HAVE A SALTWATER POOL, the way you maintain your pool will be a little different. You will be looking for different chemistry readings than freshwater pools will, and the way you balance your water will be slightly different, too. In this chapter, we are going to discuss the advantages and disadvantages of saltwater pools and everything you need to know to properly maintain yours if this is the route you choose to go.

ADVANTAGES AND DISADVANTAGES OF SALTWATER POOLS

There are many advantages and disadvantages to saltwater pools. Often, people choose saltwater pools because they have a more natural chemistry to them and do not require as many chemicals to maintain. Below is a more exhaustive list of the pros and cons of saltwater pools.

Pros of Saltwater Pools

- Saltwater is soft on your eyes and skin
- Less maintenance than chlorine pools
- Don't have to store chlorine at home
- More cost-effective over time

Cons of Saltwater Pools

- Saltwater pools cost more to set up
- You must use expert technicians for repairs
- Salt can damage pool mechanisms
- Any maintenance needed is typically not doable by yourself

Because of how saltwater pools work, if you discover that your pool chemistry is off or that something isn't balanced as it should be, you need to call in a specialist. Unlike chlorine pools, you cannot simply add chemicals to balance them. An imbalance typically means something in the mechanism isn't working correctly and needs to be fixed. Fortunately, a good quality saltwater pool should not have many issues which means that they are lower maintenance for you day to day.

HOW SALTWATER POOLS WORK

Saltwater pools work by drawing on dissolved salt in the water to generate natural chlorine. The salt cell or generator uses a process known as electrolysis to break down or separate the salt in the water. This breakdown process is what produces the natural chlorine in the form of sodium hypochlorite and hypochlorous acid. These work exactly the same way as chlorine does in a standard chlorine swimming pool.

The most important difference between saltwater and non-saltwater pools is the chloramine levels. In saltwater pools, chloramine levels are lower because they are a by-product of the breakdown of matter in the pool water. Chloramines are responsible for pungent "chlorine" smells in the pool and can cause eye irritation for swimmers. Because these levels are lower in saltwater pools, the pool tends to smell nicer and is easier on the eyes of those swimming in it.

An interesting fact is that saltwater pools have substantially lower salt content than the ocean. The average residential saltwater pool will have about 2800-4200 ppm salt levels, compared to the approximately 35,000 ppm salt levels in the ocean.

MAINTAINING THE SALTWATER CHLORINE GENERATOR

Just as with every other pool, you will need to inspect and maintain the filter, pump, and skimmer in your saltwater pool. There will be another mechanism that you need to maintain, as well. That is the saltwater chlorine generator.

The saltwater chlorine generator is responsible for the process that separates the salt from the water and creates natural chlorine. These generators last from 3-7 years, depending on the quality of brand you purchase. When you need to replace the salt cell, it costs about $700-$1100. The control board can cost around $500-$900. It is possible to extend the lifespan of either by maintaining proper salt levels and only changing the cell when needed. You can also use the reverse polarity function, which helps keep everything in good working order.

The only true maintenance your salt cell needs is a regular inspection and, when necessary, cleaning to remove scale from the mechanism. Scale can build up on the salt cell and prevent it from functioning properly, meaning you would then have to replace it sooner. Regularly inspecting this piece helps you quickly identify and eliminate scale as needed, as well as book maintenance if the mechanism needs it. Properly taking care of these two factors ensures your salt cell lasts as long as possible and maintenance stays cost-effective and easy.

BALANCING THE SALTWATER CHEMISTRY

Because of how saltwater pools function, maintaining their chemistry is different from other pools. Unlike other pools, where you can simply test the chemistry and add chlorine to balance it, saltwater pools generate their own chlorine. It also keeps the chlorine levels low while still effectively keeping the pool sanitized.

When you test the chemistry levels in your saltwater pool, the readings are expected to be different. What you do about those readings is different, too. For example, in a chlorine pool, you can shock the water. In a saltwater pool, you can still shock the pool about once a month to keep it balanced, but you must be careful not to use too much chemicals in your pool or you will destroy the natural development of chlorine and chemistry that occurs within the pool itself.

It might seem obvious, but one of the most common chemicals you will add to your pool to maintain its chemistry is *salt*. Since salt is the 'fuel' behind the development of chlorine in your pool, you will need to ensure you have plenty of salt on-hand and proper salt levels in your water. You can test saltwater levels in your pool using a specific test strip. You'll want to test it at least once per month and use this to determine how much salt to add to your water if needed. Or, if your salt is too high, you might need to drain some of your water and add fresh water to dilute your salt content.

Aside from swapping salt for chlorine, most other chemicals required to maintain your pool's proper chlorine levels, pH levels, and calcium hardness levels are the same. With that being said, you will use substantially less as your pool is more likely to stay in balance and will require fewer chemicals to adjust the chemistry when it becomes unbalanced.

COMMON SALTWATER POOL MAINTENANCE ISSUES

The most common problems you are likely to run into in your saltwater pool come from the saltwater chlorine generator. Identifying these issues promptly with frequent monitoring will ensure that you can deal with them in a timely manner and avoid unnecessary expenses caused by not taking proper care of your pool.

In general, there are six common issues you are likely to run into that can be caused by your saltwater chlorine generator. We will discuss each one in greater detail below.

Problem 1: Skin & Eye Irritations When Swimming

If you begin to notice skin or eye irritations when swimming in your saltwater pool, check your pools water chemistry. This is usually an indication that your pH levels are off. In rare instances, particularly if the problem persists despite managing it properly, it can indicate that the chlorinator is not working properly.

Problem 2: Corroded Handrails and Ladder Anchors

It's common for galvanized equipment to corrode within 4-5 years of being installed in your pool. The solution is to switch these out for brass anchors instead of galvanized ones. If you already have galvanized equipment in place, use a corrosion inhibitor to slow down the process of deterioration so you can get the most life out of them.

Problem 3: High Chlorine Levels in Your Pool

Occasionally, your chlorinator might be functioning improperly and could be producing far too much chlorine for your pool. Because it does not have a "chlorine smell," you might not notice this. The best way to avoid it is to check your pools chlorine levels on a weekly basis.

Problem 4: Cell Replacement Needed

Every 3-6 years, your chlorinator will need to be replaced. Although this is substantially cheaper than chlorine use, it is still a large up-front investment each time you must replace the chlorinator cell. This tends to be about $800-$1200 each time. You may be able to extend the life of your chlorinator with proper annual maintenance.

Problem 5: Auto Covers Being Affected

If you have an automatic cover for your pool, salt water

chlorine generators can corrode the metal components of this equipment. Regularly rinsing the metal components with fresh water is an important way to avoid having salt water sit on your metal for too long. This way, you can avoid premature corrosion and costly replacements.

Problem 6: Corroded Vinyl Liner in Pool Basin

Any pool with vinyl liners and metal walls can be affected by corrosion in a saltwater pool, regardless of whether they're in-ground or above ground. While many modern developers are using special polymer/plastic walls to avoid corrosion, it is still an issue for some swimming pools. If you build a saltwater pool with a vinyl liner or metal walls, assume that corrosion will become an issue at some point and replacements will be needed. If you are building a saltwater pool from scratch, opt for more durable polymer or plastic walls to avoid corrosion of your pool's basin. If you suspect corrosion of the basin, it may be time to call a pool company and have your liners replace for a more durable material.

CHAPTER 7
PREPARING YOUR POOL FOR THE WINTER SEASON

WINTERIZING your pool is an essential part of keeping your swimming pool safe during the off-season so that you can enjoy it again during favorable seasons. In most places, swimming pools cannot be used during the fall and winter because it is too cold to swim. Further, the cold temperatures can cause problems with the motors, filters, and other components of the swimming pool. Simply draining the pool, or leaving it as is, is not enough. This will cause damage to your pool. Properly preparing the components for winter will ensure that the cold temperatures don't damage the equipment so you can enjoy it again the following season.

There are seven important steps to follow when you are winterizing your pool. We will cover each one below. You should begin following them as soon as the weather starts to drop below 22C or 71F

STEP ONE: REMOVE ACCESSORIES

Always begin by removing the accessories from your pool, hosing them off so they're clean, then allowing them to dry completely so they can be stored indoors or in a shed for the winter. This includes the skimmer baskets, ladders, steps, cleaners, and solar blankets if you use them.

STEP TWO: DEEP CLEANING

Next, deep clean the pool itself. You want to remove as much dirt, silt, and other debris as possible so it doesn't imbalance your water chemistry and create problems over winter. Wipe down everything in your pool before using the skimmer basket to remove debris from the surface and the pool vacuum to remove anything that has sunk to the pool floor.

STEP THREE: BALANCE WATER CHEMISTRY

About one week before you officially close your pool for the season, balance your water chemistry properly. Get the alkalinity between 80 and 150 ppm, pH between 7.2 and 7.6 ppm, and calcium hardness between 175 and 225 ppm for a chlorine pool. You should also have the chlorine between 1 and 3 ppm. It is essential that you get properly balanced water chemistry before you do anything, so test and adjust as needed until you have the best possible water chemistry in your pool.

STEP FOUR: LOWER WATER LEVEL

Many people think you need your water completely drained from your pool for the season, but that's not quite true. If you use a skimmer cover *and* your water won't freeze over winter because you live in a warmer climate, you can leave your pool water as is. If you are not using a skimmer cover, or if you live in an area where the water will freeze, you need to drain some of your pool water.

On pools that have mesh covers, drain the water to about a foot below the skimmers. If you have a solid cover, drain it to about half a foot below the skimmers. This process can take time depending on how you're draining your pool water, so be ready for the work involved.

STEP FIVE: DRAIN AND STORE EQUIPMENT

Next, you need to drain, clean, dry, and store the equipment on your pool so the water inside of it doesn't expand as it cools down or freezes. If water inside of your equipment expands, it will damage your equipment. You can clear the pool lines using a blower and then insert expansion plugs into them to avoid more water finding their way into the lines. A bit of antifreeze made specifically for pools can also be run through the lines to avoid pipes bursting throughout the winter.

In addition to your pool lines, you need to drain every filter, pump, and heater in the pool. Most of these should have built-in drain plugs so the process should be fairly straightforward.

If possible, store all of your equipment indoors or in a

heated garage or shed to avoid them from being damaged due to cold weather.

STEP SIX: ADD SHOCK AND ALGAECIDE

Before you cover the pool, add shock and algaecide. The shock will kill any undesirable bacteria while the algaecide will kill algae spores. This may need to be done a few days before you cover the pool depending on what brand you use. Follow the exact instructions on the package of the products you purchase and always evenly distribute them around the pool, rather than just pouring them directly into one spot. If you use chlorinated shock, never use it at the same time as algaecide, as this can create a chlorine gas that is dangerous when inhaled.

STEP SEVEN: COVER THE POOL

Lastly, you need to cover up your pool. There are two types of covers you might use. One is a safety cover, the other is a winter cover. Safety covers must always be anchored down when you use them. They are beneficial because they protect your water from debris and they are also installed in such a way that they protect people or animals from accidentally falling into the water and either drowning or becoming hypothermic. Winter covers do not offer as much protection, but they are easier to install and tend to be cheaper to purchase. Regardless of which pool cover you choose to use, always make sure it is the right size, fits snugly around your pool, has no damage to it, and is installed properly per the instructions of the liner you purchased.

CHAPTER 8
ALGAE GROWTH CONTROL IN POOLS

ALGAE IS a common cause for concern in residential swimming pools. Particularly because they are exposed to sunlight, these pools are more at risk of developing it. Algae can turn your pool green, or it can cause cloudy water. Regardless, you will need to know how to understand its growth, identify it, prevent it, and treat it when it strikes your pool. Yes, I said 'when' not 'if' because virtually every pool will deal with some degree of an algae problem at some point. No matter how meticulous you are with water chemistry and pool care, this can be a problem for you.

UNDERSTANDING ALGAE GROWTH IN POOLS

Algae most commonly occurs when low or inconsistent chlorine levels occur. It can also be caused by faulty pool filtration or poor water circulation. Keeping algae out of your pool requires regular pool maintenance, especially as it pertains to chlorine levels.

Algae grows when spores feed on sunlight and bacteria

within the water, allowing it to flourish. Algae blooms are slimy and can turn the water itself green while also clinging to equipment within the water making it harder to remove.

Most algae is not dangerous but it is not advisable to swim in a pool that has algae growth in it because there could be other harmful elements in the water chemistry that make it unsafe for swimming. You should always thoroughly treat any algae in your pool and allow your water to stabilize after treatment before swimming in it again.

TYPES OF POOL ALGAE (AND HOW TO TREAT THEM)

There are three types of pool algae you need to know about. They include green algae, mustard algae, and black algae. All three are generally treated in the same way, though how they present and how easy they are to treat is a different story.

Green algae is the most common algae in pools. You can typically identify this type of algae in your pool before the water even really turns green because it turns the surface of your pool slimy. Visible algae can be removed with a pool brush. Shocking the pool will then help prevent the algae from coming back.

Mustard algae has a much slower growth rate but is incredibly difficult to remove from your pool. You will need to wipe the algae off the surfaces of your pool then use Super-Shock to kill the algae spores. This type of algae grows in two layers so when you wipe it off you will only remove the top layer. The bottom layer will then be exposed and treated with the Super-Shock.

Black algae is the worst of all the algae types because it grows deep into liners and can damage the structural integrity of your pool. If you notice black dots growing on the bottom or walls of your pool, that is a good sign that you have black algae growing in it. Blackspot remover is a special type of algaecide that will kill this particular type of algae and prevent it from causing damage to your pool.

PREVENTING ALGAE GROWTH IN POOLS

Avoiding algae growth in your pool requires you to regularly check your pool chemistry and keep it balanced. Imbalanced pool chemistry is what allows algae spores to begin growing and take root in your pool. If you are consistently monitoring chlorine levels and pH levels, and if you keep your equipment in good working order so water filters and circulates properly, you are unlikely to have any substantial issues with your water.

Be sure to regularly inspect your pool, as well, for the look and feel of algae. The moment you notice any, treat it properly to avoid it from spreading. This will ensure it doesn't do damage to either your water chemistry or your pools equipment.

CHAPTER 9
WEEKLY TASKS

EVERY WEEK, you need to ensure you take proper care of your pool so that it stays in good working order for years to come. Improper weekly maintenance can lead to premature breakdown of pool components, as well as costly repairs that should be otherwise unnecessary.

So far, we've discussed many of the tasks you need to do to keep your pool in good functioning order. In fact, we have discussed so many throughout this book that you might find yourself feeling a little overwhelmed. To make it easier for you, and keep all the tasks in one central place, I've compiled a list of weekly tasks you need to do to keep your pool functioning properly in this chapter.

CLEAN OUT DEBRIS AND SEDIMENT

Every week, you need to do a thorough cleaning of your pool to ensure that no debris or sediment lingers. Leaving any debris or sediment in your pool can lead to premature breakdown of parts by causing the circulation system, including the filter, pump, and pool lines to become clogged. If they become clogged and you attempt to run them, or if they are run when they are partially clogged, this can cause the parts to breakdown.

Furthermore, excessive debris and sediment in your pool will negatively impact your water chemistry. Keeping your pool clean ensures that you do not have to use as many chemicals to balance your pool chemistry, because you do not have as many contaminants causing the chemistry to become unbalanced.

To clean your pool, first skim any leaves and debris off the surface. This should always be the first step as it will avoid surface-level debris from clogging up your additional cleaning tools, such as your pool vacuum or your brush.

Once you have skimmed the surface, brush the sediment from your pool. Wipe down the sides, the ladder, steps, any accessories you have in your pool, and the bottom of your pool. Brushing the entirety of your pool ensures that any debris or sediment that has managed to cling to your pool equipment will be knocked free and can be removed by the filters or the vacuum.

The final step in cleaning debris and sediment from your pool should be vacuuming. This way, you can pick up anything that has dropped to the bottom of your pool. Doing this first can result in a large amount of debris and sediment being missed when it is knocked loose from brushing, so this should always be the last step.

CLEAN THE SKIMMER(S)

Next, you need to clean your skimmers. Skimmers are the equipment in your pool that naturally collect and remove some of the debris and sediment that falls into your pool water. Checking and cleaning them weekly ensures that your skimmers do not become overfilled and stop working. This is essential because clogged skimmers can result in clogged pool lines, filters, and pumps.

If you clean your skimmers once per week and notice that they seem to be filling up quite a bit in that time, it is worth it to switch to cleaning it twice every week. This way, you are not at risk of them becoming overfilled and causing problems for the expensive equipment that keeps your pool running.

RUN YOUR PUMP FOR CIRCULATION

Your pools circulation system is essential. It is responsible for keeping the water from getting stagnant. It helps keep debris and sediment out of your pool, helps chemicals circulate, and prevents bacteria from growing in the water. Keeping it running properly is essential.

You should be running your pump long enough each day that the contents of your entire pool has circulated adequately to ensure it remains clear and safe to swim in. Generally, this means you want to leave it running for 8 hours. However, the range can be anywhere from 6-12 hours. Your pool should have instructions on this. If it does not, a professional or a calculator online can help you determine what the flow rate of your pump is and how long it needs to be run for a pool the size of yours.

Just because your pump needs to run this long doesn't mean it should be run consecutively. While you can, it is cheaper to break up your pump time so that you are running it during non-peak hours. This could mean running half of your hours early in the morning and half late at night, for example. On particularly hot days when the pool has high UV exposure, running your pump is ideal as it helps keep the chlorine working properly during those hours.

CHECK FILTER AND BACKWASH

There are three types of filters that your pool might have. It could have a sand filter, a cartridge, filter, or a vertical grid DE filter. Each of these filters has different cleaning requirements. Further, different manufacturers might have different cleaning requirements. You will want to read the directions to better understand the maintenance protocol for your unique filter.

Regardless of which filter you have, you need to check it weekly to ensure that you thoroughly remove any debris that has gathered in it. You can then do any maintenance tasks that the manual might request of you, too.

If you find that your filter is particularly dirty, backwashing it is a good way to remove sediment and debris from it. This is most likely needed when the pool has been used a lot, as this is when you are more likely to find a lot of debris in the pool.

TEST WATER AND ADJUST CHEMISTRY

Finally, you need to test your water chemistry and adjust it as needed. Generally, chemicals are added to the pool every day to keep it in good balance. These include different types of disinfectants and sanitizers that ensure no bacteria grows within your pool. If you do not use your pool as often, and if the water generally stays clean and free of debris, you might only need to add these chemicals on a weekly basis.

Check with your unique chemical instructions, as each manufacturer has different requirements. Some are stronger and only need to be used on a weekly basis while others need to be used daily.

Typically, you will need to check and balance your chlorine levels at least weekly to ensure they remain balanced. At this time, you might also discover other imbalances that require treatment, such as with your pH levels.

Keep track of your weekly readings and treatments in a notebook so you always know what you've done to the pool. This way, you can spot trends that might indicate the growth of unwanted bacteria or the disintegration of pool equipment. You can also use these to determine what worked last time your pool was imbalanced so you have an idea of what to do anytime your pool becomes imbalanced in the future.

CHAPTER 10
OPTIMIZING POOL MAINTENANCE FOR ENERGY EFFICIENCY

MAXIMIZING Energy Efficiency in Pool Maintenance

In this chapter, we will cover ways to maximize energy efficiency in pool maintenance. Proper energy management can significantly lower your pool's operating costs and environmental impact. We will discuss various energy-saving techniques, equipment, and maintenance practices to help you achieve a crystal-clear pool with minimal effort and energy consumption.

1. Energy-Efficient Pool Pumps

Switching to an energy-efficient pool pump can reduce your pool's energy consumption by up to 65%. Look for a variable-speed or two-speed pump, which allows you to adjust the speed based on your pool's specific needs. Variable-speed pumps are more energy-efficient and quieter compared to traditional single-speed pumps.

2. Optimal Pump Operating Time

Run your pool pump during off-peak hours when electricity rates are lower, usually early in the morning or late at night. Experiment with running the pump for shorter periods to find the optimal operating time that maintains water clarity without wasting energy.

3. Properly Sizing Pool Equipment

Ensure that your pool equipment is appropriately sized for your pool. Oversized pumps, filters, and heaters can consume more energy than necessary. Consult a pool professional to determine the correct equipment size for your pool.

4. Regularly Clean and Maintain Equipment

Regularly cleaning and maintaining your pool equipment can improve energy efficiency. A clean filter will reduce the load on your pump, which in turn reduces energy consumption. Make sure to clean your filter, skimmer, and pump baskets regularly and replace them when necessary.

5. Use a Pool Cover

Using a pool cover can significantly reduce energy consumption by retaining heat and reducing evaporation. A pool cover also helps to keep debris out of the pool, reducing the need for cleaning and filtration.

6. Efficient Pool Heating Options

Consider using solar pool heaters or heat pumps to heat your pool more efficiently. Solar pool heaters use the sun's energy to heat the water, while heat pumps transfer heat from the air to the pool water. Both options are more energy-efficient than gas or electric heaters.

7. Optimize Water Circulation

Ensure that your pool's water circulation is optimized by positioning the return jets to create a uniform flow of water. This helps to distribute the chemicals evenly throughout the pool and prevents dead spots where algae can grow.

8. LED Pool Lighting

Switch to LED pool lights, which are more energy-efficient and have a longer lifespan compared to traditional incandescent or halogen bulbs. LED lights also offer more vibrant colors and can be controlled remotely for added convenience.

9. Regularly Check for Leaks

A leaking pool can lead to significant water and energy waste. Regularly inspect your pool for signs of leaks and promptly address any issues you find.

10. Plant Windbreaks

Planting windbreaks around your pool can reduce evaporation and heat loss by blocking wind. Consider planting trees or installing fences to create a barrier that will help conserve energy.

11. Educate Pool Users

Educate your family and guests on energy-efficient pool practices, such as using the pool cover, keeping the pool clean, and turning off unnecessary pool equipment when not in use.

By implementing these energy-saving techniques and regularly maintaining your pool, you can achieve a crystal-clear pool while minimizing your energy consumption and operating costs. This not only benefits your wallet but also reduces your environmental impact, allowing you to enjoy your pool with peace of mind.

CHAPTER 11
SEASONAL POOL CARE: MAINTAINING YOUR POOL THROUGHOUT THE YEAR

YOU MIGHT BE SURPRISED to learn that opening your pool requires just as much effort as closing it. In Chapter 7 we talked about winterizing your pool. Now, we are going to talk about how to properly open your pool for the season, as well as mid-summer maintenance and winter tasks you should engage with to ensure your pool remains functional all year long.

OPENING YOUR POOL FOR THE SEASON

In the spring, when you are ready to open your pool for the season, there are six essential steps you must take to ensure it is ready and safe to swim in.

Step One: Clean Debris And Inspect Deck Furniture

The first step is to sweep any leaves and debris away from the sides of the pool and do a visual inspection for any wear and tear on the sides of the pool or deck furniture. This will ensure that you do not accidentally introduce any debris to the pool when you open it, and that you can properly maintain anything that may have become damaged over the winter.

Step Two: Inventory Your Pool Chemicals

Inventory your pool chemicals before you draw the cover on the pool. This way, you know what you have and you can begin treating the water as soon as you open your pool for the season. This ensures bacteria and algae do not have a head-start when you first pull the cover off.

You should have:

- A pool test kit
- Chlorine
- Shock treatment
- pH Adjusters
- Algaecide treatment
- Filter cleaner

Step Three: Remove The Cover

Next, draw the cover off. Begin by using a cover pump to remove any water from the surface, as well as any debris that has collected. Then, carefully pull it back to avoid dropping any further debris in the pool.

Step Four: Inspect The Pool

Once the cover is off, inspect the pool. Remove winterizing plugs, inspect the filter and pump, reinstall any underwater lights you may have removed, inspect the basin, and check the pool lines. You want to ensure everything is in good working order before you do anything further.

Step Five: Fill The Pool And Clean It

If everything looks good, you can fill your pool to the halfway point of your waterline tile, or the middle of your skimmer opening. Then, give your pool a good cleaning following the cleaning steps in Chapter 9.

Step Six: Filter And Test The Water

With everything clean, your pool is ready to be turned on. Turn on the filter then test your water and balance the water chemistry so it is safe to swim in. If you are going to be using it a lot, ensure you have plenty of chemicals for the season as well as a good cleaning schedule in place right from the start of the season. This way, your pool is ready for heavy use.

SUMMER MAINTENANCE TASKS

About halfway into the summer, or once per month throughout the summer if you are using your pool often, you should do a full inspection of the pool to ensure everything is in good working order.

Check the pump, filter, pool lines, skimmer baskets, ladders, steps, chemical feeders, basin, and everything else associated with your pool. If you have accessories like floaties or toys, this is a good time to inspect those, too.

You want to ensure that everything is in good working

order *and* that it is free of debris and sediment. For example, pool floaties can become breeding grounds for bacteria and algae. Properly rinsing them off weekly and inspecting them monthly to ensure they aren't gathering dirt around their corners, plugs, or other areas ensures they are not introducing any unwanted contaminants to your water.

WINTER MAINTENANCE TASKS

You might think that in the middle of winter you can just ignore your pool for the entire season. If you live in a particularly cold climate and your pool is covered in snow, this might not be an option. However, if you live somewhere slightly warmer and the pool is not covered in snow, or if you have thaws throughout the winter, it is a good idea to pull the cover back on your pool and do a good cleaning of your water.

Testing and treating your water to maintain good chemistry throughout the winter season will make reopening your pool in the spring much easier, too. If your water has a frozen surface, however, it is better to just leave it alone to avoid causing any damage to your basin. Attempting to crack open the ice could result in you accidentally tearing a hole in your liner which would lead to a costly repair.

CHAPTER 12
ECO-FRIENDLY PRACTICES FOR POOL MAINTENANCE

FINALLY IN THIS LAST CHAPTER, we will explore eco-friendly pool maintenance practices that can help reduce your pool's environmental impact while still maintaining a clean and healthy swimming environment. By adopting these sustainable practices, you can enjoy your pool with the added satisfaction of knowing that you're doing your part in preserving the environment.

1. Use Natural and Eco-Friendly Pool Chemicals

Traditional pool chemicals can be harmful to the environment and pose health risks for swimmers. Consider switching to natural and eco-friendly alternatives that are gentler on the environment and human health. For example, using mineral sanitizers like copper and silver ions or enzyme-based pool treatments can reduce your reliance on harsh chemicals like chlorine.

2. Install a Natural Filtration System

Natural filtration systems, such as a poolside bog or a regeneration zone, use plants to filter and clean pool water. These systems mimic natural ecosystems and can be an excellent eco-friendly alternative to traditional pool filters. They require less energy and fewer chemicals while providing a unique and aesthetically pleasing environment.

3. Adopt a Solar-Powered Pool System

Harnessing the power of the sun can significantly reduce your pool's energy consumption. Installing solar panels to power your pool's pump, heater, and lighting can be an effective way to reduce your pool's carbon footprint. Additionally, consider investing in a solar pool cover to retain heat, minimize evaporation, and decrease the need for heating.

4. Conserve Water

Water conservation is crucial in maintaining an eco-friendly pool. Regularly check for leaks, use a pool cover to reduce evaporation, and avoid overfilling the pool to minimize water waste. When backwashing your filter, consider reusing the water for irrigation or cleaning purposes instead of discharging it into the sewer system.

5. Encourage Natural Pest Control

Instead of relying on chemical treatments to control pests around your pool, adopt natural pest control methods. Encourage beneficial insects, such as ladybugs and lacewings, by planting flowers and shrubs that attract them. These insects will help control pests like mosquitoes and flies, reducing the need for chemical insecticides.

6. Install a Rainwater Harvesting System

Collecting rainwater to use in your pool is an excellent way to conserve water and reduce your environmental impact. Install a rainwater harvesting system to collect runoff from your roof and divert it to your pool. This can help maintain your pool's water level and reduce your reliance on municipal water sources.

7. Choose Eco-Friendly Pool Construction Materials

If you're building or renovating your pool, consider using eco-friendly materials that have a lower environmental impact. For example, opt for a natural stone or recycled glass pool finish instead of traditional plaster. Choose sustainable decking materials like composite or responsibly sourced wood.

8. Practice Responsible Pool Landscaping

Incorporate native plants and drought-tolerant species in your pool landscaping to conserve water and create a more sustainable environment. These plants require less water and maintenance, reducing your overall resource consumption. Additionally, choose permeable surfaces for your pool deck to reduce runoff and prevent soil erosion.

9. Minimize Noise Pollution

Pool equipment, such as pumps and filters, can generate noise pollution that affects both humans and wildlife. Choose quiet, energy-efficient equipment, and consider installing noise-reducing barriers or enclosures to minimize the impact of noise on your surroundings.

10. Educate and Involve Pool Users

Inform your family members and guests about your eco-friendly pool maintenance practices and encourage them to participate. Share the importance of conserving water, using natural alternatives to chemicals, and maintaining a clean pool environment. By fostering a sense of shared responsibility, you can create a more sustainable and enjoyable pool experience for everyone.

By adopting these eco-friendly pool maintenance practices, you can create a more sustainable and environmentally friendly swimming environment. Not only will these measures help reduce your pool's environmental impact, but they will also contribute to a healthier and more enjoyable swimming experience for you, your family, and your guests. Embracing sustainable pool maintenance practices demonstrates your commitment to preserving the environment and promoting a greener future.

CONCLUSION

As we reach the end of this comprehensive guide on pool maintenance, it's essential to reflect on the knowledge you've gained and the steps you can take to maintain a crystal-clear and healthy pool all season long. Proper pool maintenance not only ensures a safe and enjoyable swimming experience for you, your family, and your guests but also helps extend the life of your pool and its components, saving you time, effort, and money in the long run.

Throughout this book, we have covered various aspects of pool maintenance, starting from understanding the basics and components of a swimming pool, to learning about different types of pools and pool maintenance technologies. We have also explored essential pool maintenance equipment and chemicals, routine pool maintenance tasks, and troubleshooting common pool problems. You have gained insights into advanced pool maintenance techniques, salt-water pool maintenance, winterizing your pool, algae control, weekly and seasonal care, and environmentally friendly pool maintenance practices.

CONCLUSION

As you embark on your pool maintenance journey, remember that consistency and attention to detail are crucial. Develop a routine that works best for you and your specific pool, and stick to it. Regularly monitor your pool's water chemistry, equipment, and cleanliness to prevent issues before they escalate into more significant problems.

Consider adopting energy-efficient and eco-friendly practices to reduce your pool's environmental impact and operating costs. By implementing sustainable pool maintenance techniques, you contribute to preserving the environment and promoting a greener future. This not only benefits you and your wallet but also ensures a healthier planet for future generations.

As you progress in your pool maintenance journey, don't hesitate to consult with pool professionals or fellow pool owners for advice and guidance. Continuous learning and staying up-to-date on the latest pool maintenance technologies, products, and best practices can help you refine your skills and optimize your pool maintenance routine.

Remember that every pool is unique, and what works for one may not work for another. Experiment with different approaches and techniques to find what works best for your specific pool and needs. Be patient and allow yourself time to learn, adapt, and improve your pool maintenance skills. With time and experience, you will become more confident in your abilities, and maintaining your pool will become second nature.

In summary, maintaining a crystal-clear pool requires dedication, knowledge, and the right equipment. By following the guidance provided in this book, you can become proficient in pool maintenance, ensuring a safe and enjoyable swimming experience for everyone who uses your pool. While pool maintenance can be challenging at times, it can also be incredibly rewarding, as you see the results of your efforts in the form of a sparkling clean and inviting pool.

As you continue to grow and refine your pool maintenance skills, remember that your ultimate goal is to create a safe, healthy, and enjoyable environment for yourself, your family, and your guests. By investing time and effort into pool maintenance, you are investing in countless hours of relaxation, fun, and memories that will last a lifetime.

Thank you for joining us on this journey through the world of pool maintenance. We hope that this guide has provided you with the knowledge, tools, and confidence you need to maintain your pool successfully. As you apply the lessons learned in this book, may you and your loved ones enjoy countless days of fun and relaxation in your crystal-clear pool.

AFTERWORD

Congratulations on completing **Pool Maintenance DIY Beginner's Guide** *The Art of Keeping a Crystal Clear Pool All Season Long With Minimal Effort.* This guide was designed to help you confidently look after your pool so you can enjoy a safe, healthy, and comfortable swimming season in your own backyard!

Looking after a pool might seem like a lot of work if you're new to it, but once you get into a good routine with your pool maintenance tasks, it's easy. It's important to remember that a properly maintained pool is an easy keeper. One that is neglected or not looked after will be difficult to maintain because you are regularly trying to fix what has come unbalanced. It can even be downright expensive if you end up having to replace components prematurely because of carelessness.

By following the steps in this guide, you will be able to properly maintain your pool so that it is one of the easy keepers. This will also keep your costs of running your pool as low as possible, because you are not regularly having to treat algae outbreaks or repair parts of the pool that are coming apart due to neglect.

If you have read this far, you are all ready to look after your pool like a pro! Before you go, I ask one favor: can you please review this book on the platform you purchased it from? Your honest review ensures other people know this is an excellent guide for keeping their pools, as well. It also helps me serve you better!

Thank you, and I hope you have a wonderful swimming season!

RESOURCES

- *4 tips to maintaining a safe swimming pool water level.* Kreepy Krauly. (2022, October 24).
- *7 common pool problems and how to fix them.* (n.d.).
- Fann-Im, N. (2020, July 30). *How to winterize a pool.* This Old House.
- Giovanisci, M. (2021, September 3). *How to balance the calcium hardness level in your pool.* Swim University
- Giovanisci, M. (2022, January 22). *How to raise the ph level in your pool: The easy way.* Swim University
- Harris, T. (2002, September 17). *How swimming pools work.* HowStuffWorks.
- *How to maintain a pool | lowe's.* (n.d.).
- *How to shock a pool.* The Home Depot.
- *How to test the cyanuric acid level in your pool (5 easy steps).* Poolonomics. (2023, February 3).
- Johnson, E. (2022, June 2). *How to clean your pump*

basket: Browning pools & spas: Custom inground swimming pools: Montgomery County, MD. Browning Pools & Spas.
- lpusaeditor2. (2020, September 21). *Pool maintenance 101: Water chemistry.* Leisure Pools Canada.
- M, P., Rodriguez, K. S., McLean, M., Ripkowski, G., & Novacek, L. M. (2020, March 6). *How does a saltwater pool system work?* Blue Science.
- Marketing, B. H. (2019, April 24). *Pool problems: The most common problems pool owners encounter.* Hammerhead Pools.
- Miller, A. (2020, December 16). *Pool algae – the 3 types.* Hyclor.
- Outbackp. (n.d.). *The importance of cleaning your swimming pool - 3 tips.* Outback Pools and Spas.
- *The Perfect Pool Blog.* Zodiac Blog - Swimming Pool Chemicals. (n.d.). Retrieved April 12, 2023
- *Pool water testing.* The Home Depot. (n.d.).
- Spas, B. H. P. &. (2020, February 22). *Swimming Pool Equipment: 5 technology options for Comfort & Convenience.* Swimming Pool Facts and Tips. Retrieved April 12, 2023
- Taylor, L. H. (2022, September 9). *A guide to 12 typs of swimming pools.* The Spruce. Retrieved April 12, 2023,
- *Total dissolved solids.* Total Dissolved Solids | In The Swim. (n.d.).
- *Weekly Maintenance.* Weekly Maintenance | Pool Maintenance | Support - Hayward Pool Products. (n.d.). Retrieved April 12, 2023,
- *What are the six most common salt water chlorine generator problems.* Home - 3 Day Pools. (n.d.).

- *What happens if ph is too high in a pool?* HGTV. (n.d.). Retrieved April 12, 2023
- *What happens if ph is too low in a pool? (5 nasty side effects)*. Poolonomics.

www.ingramcontent.com/pod-product-compliance
Lightning Source LLC
Chambersburg PA
CBHW072216070526
44585CB00015B/1367